THE GARDEN

ELRIC WENTZ

Copyright © 2023 by Elric A. Wentz

All rights reserved.

Monroe, NC

No parts of this publication may be reproduced, stored in a retrieval system, or transmitted in any form or by any means, electronic, mechanical, photocopying, recording, or otherwise, without the prior written permission of the author.

This book is sold subject to the condition that it shall not, by way of trade or otherwise, be lent, resold, hired out, or otherwise circulated without the author's prior consent in any form of binding or cover other than that in which it is published and without a similar condition including this condition being imposed on the subsequent purchaser. Under no circumstances may any part of this book be photocopied for resale.

This is a work of creative expression. Any similarity between the characters and situations within its pages and places or persons, living or dead, is likely co-incidental or subjective through the eye of the author, not fact. Do with that what you will.

Cover Art from Canva.com

Formatting by Corbeaux Editorial Services

For permission to reprint material please email elricwentz@gmail.com

❦ Created with Vellum

CONTENTS

1. Amor Fati — 1
2. Deja Vu — 21
3. Movies — 43
4. She! — 69
5. Big Blue — 91
6. Vici — 111

About the Author — 135

1
AMOR FATI

All of those old versions of me are dead,
And gone, and I buried them all myself
in the backyard.
You remind me that this isn't a match, no one's keeping
score, but I'm demure to the fact,
that you pull the yellow card.
A stranger borne thinking out loud,
Can't tell the people from the crowd
But I can tell the exodus
And you smell just like pixie dust.
I cross my arms and posit, "is this it for us?"
And you wonder if I still believe in fairies.

It's Autumn and the passage of time has been pervasive
on my mind. I'm 29 and finding my embers strong in
spite of my malaise. That yesteryear and the coming

days, stand in stark defiance. Your animus and my modus operandi cannot cohabitate. You carry this monkey around so we can see eye to eye; and it's a pity. It's the first week of September and I slept on this: my head was heavy, and my heart was tender, I pooled the bad blood up in a corner and made it back home in time for dinner.
The winds crept in and cooled it down.
It's Autumn and time keeps flowing and unbeknownst to me, that by the creek bed there stood a little boy with a gentle heart. Learning that sometimes to mend things, you must first take them apart.

What my dad taught me:
was that a man is only here for so long and what he contributes to make the world more beautiful is his own to discern,
And same goes for me when it is my turn.

This is my malady
Milady
This is reality, baby
With a stream of thoughts
Like a three-ring circus
And a mouth like a shotgun.
That is a monstrosity
Mon Cheri
The spread that separates us from we.
Don't wrest with my pedantry,
There is better use to your time:
We'll come back to this place like
Clockwork, Clementine.

A Season in Heaven

If I must, since you pried,
It may now seem like an illusion,
A heaven that ivy tried to hide,
Embrazened by diffusion.
When I capitulated
I'd strike a match
Lit a wick, a lick of flame,
When you couldn't be manipulated,
And could hardly be named!

I had seven kinds of whimsy
Pockets effuse with riches
Sweet and penniless.
And everyone was there,
and everyone walked
side by side,
like they were the same
in God's eyes.

It wasn't too far away,
That the tower's tongue flailed wildly.
And ours is king, that patently disarms
Patiently smiting or smiling.
Out of the woods and in the clear,
Be still and rest your soul here.

I feel like the whole time that
we never stopped sleeping,
We never stopped smiling,
we are what we are seeking.
And there's no hiding,
and there is no peeking.
We do it out of faith.

This clandestine destiny
Isn't what I hoped it'd be
And you're doing your thing
You're dreaming your dreams.
I reckoned for a millennia
I left honest, I felt clean
Rich as a plum
As the juice streams down your cheeks.

I never saw idle hands. I never saw bones,
I never saw the queue to cast the first stone.
A heaven that ivy tried to hide,
Emboldened by creatures, that tried!
See-
Heaven, sometimes,
is like a roller coaster ride,
Everybody wants to go
but nobody wants to die.

Morning glory morning glory,
close to the ground,
Splay out the blue petals,
soon they'll turn brown.
Where are you, where are you going?
Flung this way and that
by the wind
So, the seeds will soon need sewing
And all of the sunlight
you can lend.

The beautiful are most certainly damned.
You can cast the good against the evil.
The corridors are queued up & quite crammed.
But there's still the traditional upheaval
They'll try to buy out
every seat of the committee.
Disposed to casual recklessness
and to callous erasure.
Declare your downfall a
Self-fulfilling prophecy.
As they wrest the halos from Mother Nature;
And relegate echoes to fault lines;
They'll take everything you've ever looked forward to-
and put it all far behind.
As you answer the questions
in the back of your mind- Infini -

The beautiful are most assuredly damned
And I for one,
would not choose to save them.

Dispel the gentle horrors
Knelt by the hung jurors
Make men of these mice
Let lesser men be sworn thin
Forfeit your secrets,
don't fret about the wretched, the untrue
In the lonely torpid moments,
When your eyes want to hide,
Propel me to your craterous dark side-
And all of the world, when you just
Shave it down to the bone:
You always say you came into this life alone —
It would be a shame
to leave it in such a way.

For the young and young at heart,
Creeping up to your favorite part.
Behold a bloom
a petal of a flower
Bronzed in blues
and never to sour,
A single petal; sleep to settle.
A world over left to discover and scour –
Never let anyone dull your sparkle:
Glimmer on soft hearted
Love by design,
And don't let those hardened hearts
Contort your mind.
Do as children do, act like children act
Rush toward Blythe & reckless & without maps.

Because in the end, everyone's afraid of heights.

Scattered between
north and south
From knowing my worth
And hearing your mouth
Strewn between
East and west
From being at peace,
to being my best.

Stars spattered in a sea of obsidian,
She shifted her weight
There weren't any arms on her chair
Her mind posited me a revelator
And her thoughts weren't so simple to sate,
As I.

And clouds, in spite of my comfort,

Swell with pain, and despair,
That we inconsolably sire
Will spill over leaving us wondering,
Wounded and wet.

Though the white mountain flowers may be weeds
I have fashioned a crown out of dandelion
seeds.

You may dream marvelous, in marble
Ivory, and alabaster.
Carved of both, or out of either,
Hope or disaster.

You may strut in sewn satin, or silk,
Chiffons or chenilles.
Dare you look at the boys &
see them bend to your will.

(Time and again
I treat these silver
filigreed thoughts
like a tourist)
make an effigy
of yesterday and
strive not to bore us.

You may desire a way, or even
Know just what you mean
But ambition, tis latent decisions,
Waiting to be seen.

Sometimes I feel so pointless
Sometimes I feel so downtrodden
Sometimes I feel appointed
To stand on a pillow of cotton:
Sipping on sweet disappointment.

This morn I caught my lover's breath
She held to the sea for all its depth
Spread eagle in a field filled with daffodils
She rounds up the agents of time, and of ills
Casts them towards the sun without indecision
A truer thought never stirred or awoken.
You're a contradiction by definition
Once borne and never broken:
In the morning, I'll catch your glory.
And casually, slowly, distill the divinity
In so much from
How much I adore thee.

2
DEJA VU

Subsequent to the possession of my mind.
I drifted, nay
Wandered, they
Wondered, and
Sifted, sand—
Every grain, in the hourglass slips, drips, and shifts,
Into the great expanse, bespattered, until they twinkle, twinkle,
and leave enough room for rain to come back out:
Which Dampens my collar,
Tamps down my callousness,
And whets my curiosity.

I heard a murmur that may have been a commotion —
From whence it was, for there it were,
it did and does or do, assured;
and since it occurred, under my watch,
I scratched the surface and purchased a tour.

I frequented sheds where shades were kept
I dried the tears that the muses had wept
I was like clay fresh for the kiln, soon immutable, still malleable,
Where truth could live with right or wrong,
and only the fallacious was fallible.

In nothing, and I weighed less than a feather
I never gave a moment to check the weather
And I fit in nothing,
and my means are but a foot in a glove.
With the blank expression of love,
With the faint apparition of yesterday's,
and at the crossroads of time and the human face of calamity.
Of a world we lie too still to chase,
A world we lose when we awake,
And a patience not lessened with today's urgency.
That's when I found my mind, meandering;
Replete with candor, and hungry for answering,
And a thirst no thought could glut.

Hope springs eternal and the fountain overfloweth.
After the first frost of fall, the orchids still groweth.
And when the petals flower,
they will only need to be their beauty
and assuage your doubts.

The sunshine supplants the hues,
With a feeling of elation and
Waiting for my cues.
For figment or for fiction,
and not for a fact I'd listen
Hoping to be delivered
to the right decision.
Praying for another spring to glisten.

I see no reason
Not to end your suffering
I need no excuse
Not to call it my own.
And upon your coffin
I'll watch them shoveling,
File out of the pews,
File the innocence loaned.
You either view life as a game
Or a piece of art.
You can't appreciate both
the right way with those monikers.
To grow old —
To grow fat —
To grow certain
That you acknowledge her
& nothing else so matters.

The tyranny of small things.
The Mecca of my mind has Atrophied
The lick of honey in your iris,
The rear view and the nectar of Osiris.
I thought, no dreamt, I saw you standing,
Re-creating the moon landing,
Lavinia Fisher lazily fanning,
The flames I've tasked myself to stoke.

When the geyser of inspiration dried up for the muses,
I tell them about you.
Show them portraits and poems to
prove you're even real.

We offer these tributes to Neptune,
Spot mermaids along the horizon.
And beneath waves, a pedant's boon,
And a layman's loot —
Feuds that foisted Athena's boot.
The scrap yard was next to the graveyard & you said
they were basically the same.
And the pool is full,
Where even fools have pull,
The new normal is incorrigible
And nothing really horrible
Ever happens.
While the true trove is sunk,
Whisked away by sand, but still coveted.

The Rhythms of the Young

She doesn't know about Missingno's,
She only loves the rain for the after-bows.
Tales of Middle Carolina Almanacs,
Makes her remind me of the facts-
That the suns coming up.
...Zzz...
We've got all the time
...
Tell it till it's to the top of your lungs
And hear the rhythms of the young.

And through the after-work din
and purposeless chatter
I keep thinking there can be nothing sadder
And chide myself for my pomp.
I think of cannabis-induced lung transplants
And insufferable white picket fence lunatics —
Dense and frenetic,

Assembling Skeletons in the attic,
Reminiscing about
Front door politics.
I've been holding back lately
You keep in touch when ya runnin' on empty.
I've been orbiting society
Trying to find purchase with my extremities.
...
Tell it till it's to the top of your lungs
And recite to me, the rhythms of the young.

Already seen, already known, already lived.

From for, to forte, to fortitude
is quite the evolution —
laid splayed tracing the stars
that outline our only solution.
We measure the tigers
by the length of their teeth;
And we know the flavor of life
is most palatable.
Scribbled upon your heart,
whet with liquid relief —
Both Vacuous and Invaluable.
You can't wizen up to the lives
that you already knew —
Deja Vu Deja Su Deja Vecu.

Do not be defeated,
Do not let them get to you.
They try to get me
Too.

Take your leave, sadness,
And answer to the mundane.
There's no foothold for you here.
I sometimes wish that Georgia,
Would make restless legs sit still.

Make yours my lot for madness,
There's no corner left to fear —
I can't help but wonder
if the world has changed.
Shack up at the usual address,
Or answer to the mundane
(And we both know
Neither is Providence for Rubber Tramps)
Remote from consequence.
(And sailors make for a poor fence.)

Hellenistically sick
And prone to pleasure
We do our best work
Whilst we toil in leisure.

We are the paper tears,
We are the misprints
We are the sad truths;
Satisfyingly diffident
&
Comfortably uncouth.
In search of free will,
And to shake the
stars from our bones —
'Cuz they don't know
the meanin' of bein' Alone
Like it's easy.

Juniper leaves and Jennifer, doll —
Will either still be around by fall?
I will pull you from the everyday wreckage
I will be a beacon & relay the message.
This isn't rubbish, this is existence!
Carve out the path of least resistance.
Jet out to the blue abyss
That's calling me back once again
And Appreciate...
A Calm in nature's kindness
Reminds me of my wildness
The Creek's steady trickle, mindless.
As Effortless
as
the
Trees.

You ran out of gas on the detour
Your pedals have been glued to the floor
You don't know what you're driving towards,
But that's life,
It's always moving forward.
He walked around with his hand on her back
So it looked like he held her by knife point
And she was merely playing out the part.
But that was prior to the fire
And after the laughter —
I only dream in dopamine.

I no longer measure my days in dirty dishes.
I filter my heart through these little trinkets.
I draw your cheek near and lift your chin up,
Your eyes glisten like distant
lanterns every Christmas.

There is another story going on,
I want to be on the side that has won.
Venus sits on a shelf
supervising the moon;
She shamefully draws the shades for cover.

It's the news heard the whole world over
It's the two-for-one special at the local Kroger.
I sit and I ponder over my morning coffee,
That you don't do to me,
what Obama did to Gaddafi.

And I'll be your Deja Vu,
And you will be my turn of the screw.

I don't want to be in your wake.

We are the cadence of fae and moon beams
As silver screens pollute self-assured streams.
We are the dialects of lay gods —
What a horrible name for such a lovely thing —
When the closing bells toll, what could they bring?

Well, I
Saw the sun and I
told her that without her
the world would be much colder.

& I
Product of the moon
Wary of recognition
Aware embers still smolder.

The looms of fate have spun us fruits

Of Epicureanism in its day, to bloom.
Shake your
Head, hands, and hips
Just please do something I can't predict.

3
MOVIES

Movies

Movie lines stick in my mind.
She was aiding and embedding a bevy of stars, some were bright and gleaming, and others were keeping to themselves as they were slowly dancing. She didn't know what was going on. In her head, in her town, or God forbid, even in her fiction.

"I'll have what she's having."

But what she did know shined like diamonds under firelight or in cell phone glow, with the stringency of coral and the efficacy of coal miners. "Are you sure? Because I like the black." I recoil with a flinch and have lived enough to nod affirmation. She rolled her eyes perfunctorily— they always got dry— and rapped against the skin of the drum with her fingertips, inaudibly.

"Frankly my dear, I don't give a damn."

She is, in principle, an Aries heiress that makes me question my footing as of late. I step on firm ground and think maybe it'll all fall out beneath. "... you're talking. The things... you are dreaming points..." My focus came and went and spent and never once rescinded, but I was never once removed. Just sometimes watching things happen from behind the projector.

"Here's looking at you, kid."

The archivists of my mind had no answer, and my memory was checkered with idyllic even-falls and the headwinds of doubt, that could draw no conclusion on me.
I straightened down and lit my penultimate cigarette, slightly bent, and soaked up the afternoon sun, and became bent on understanding how a person can go their lives believing the contents of their whole being could fit in a bill fold. "A consequence of fallacy, imbued in deception, and foisted on ..."

"Thanks," I reach for my scarf and find it a fool's errand. The goal is to make our ideas ideal, and our ideologies real.

She preached the language of birds and, inculpated by every bead of sweat, and her laugh was always wry, and her nose was often wrinkled.
"You don't understand."

This makes me puke.

"Do you measure a man by his mettle or his merit? Some men are not a monster made until you see the whites of their eyes, some until you hear the blacks of their souls." And on and on and on. I never once understood, until the credits rolled.

I love your alacrity, because sometimes I look at you
and get giddy. I'm fifteen inches below and a thousand
miles out. Your conditioned tenacity when the A/C
finally makes it moves the clouds.
I'll enjoy myself, but I wish you would first.
I know I cultivate solitude, surly and terse.
I don't know why.

An homage to garbage.
(A bandage for the obvious.)

Believe me when I tell you
I'll take the shadows, take up the doubt,
Rain clouds pool together
Sweaty and ready for another bout.
I don't cling to you like a secret,
Burnt down like a matchstick
And flooded until someone
turned off the faucet.
The smile is not manufactured about,
it's locally sourced.
So open up and let me in,
'Cuz Jack's been hitting the bottle again.

I dig in my heels
I feel the sewing of your roots
The capillaries of your blood lines
The bright spot in your grey Monday.
You shrug your shoulders
And only look up between meals.

Columbia

I've been trying to understand you, Columbia.
There's a run in your stockings
and a seam in your dress.
And it's easy to be underneath you,
with your sun-spangled blouse,
whilst your mood is any
Caucasian's guess...
You are who you always wanted to be,
You scoff and shift the onus to me.
And though boomers will own this,
Gen Z can't take the slowness.
It's partly fabricated in an offshore factory, and washes
up, reserved, fully pernicious. Strung to this place and
beyond the sound of tired. Dew drops of yearning cling
to your freshly harvested pastures.

I've been trying to understand you, Columbia.

While another state is subliminally conquered. I've
been stuck in traffic for almost an hour. I was let down
by you and the verdict was dour. The land, of the free,
paid for, by the hour. For chrissakes.
Your irises sparkled with delight,
As the streetlights play hide and seek in them and you
make me feel temporary— momentary.

I've been trying to understand you, Columbia.
I've fled the conflagration to build the utopia. You let
billions in, beleaguered, and begrudged them all, and
charged them extra for international calls.
I've belittled the past and now I'm lost for the future;
I've been handed my bruises and dealt my sutures. Let
the bruises grow like flowers and flourish like excuses.
I'll write you again during another commercial break.
Subsidize the cable cars and marinate the steaks.
Why don't we all collectively dwell on our mistakes?
I've been trying to understand you, Columbia.

I didn't hurt anyone, did I? "The stock is trading higher
this hour," said I. While my heart belongs to an angel,
you decide my body belongs to you and you bank on it
not getting too old. You're indifferent that my soul
belongs to whomever when the box gets cold.
Gave up stealing to be a day trader,
I'm trying not to blur the lines
But Doctor, I Am Pagliacci,
When I return the stocks will climb.
Got a pocketful of Washingtons
Which can afford to get me nothing
but robbed.

Oh say can you see,
I've been trying to understand you.
Columbia.

Leave it to each man to
come to grip with his scruples.
May he be urbane,
May he be feudal.
Let it be to each one to
forge their own destiny.
Maybe we're hell bound!
Quite possibly heaven?
But most certainly
here.

The sun and the moon are persuading.
Press the ripened moment
(Gently misbehaving)
They trip over each other, slip inside gleefully,
Skip with plenitude and laugh
Innocuously rocking
And mockingly keep turning
Around and down, tilted by the axis
Waiting for their turn to light the way.

Growing old has to be fickle and flippant
Like tickling is fun or it just plain isn't—
It hurts like hell.
Everything has to be transactional
And somehow the sun is always in your eyes.
Growing old has to be a look
Of subtle indignation or
befuddled as the colors bleed away.
Growing old has to be a new flavor of prison
A predilection towards suspicion
of unwarranted grins.

I Look Before I Leap

I look before I leap
And the dawn capriciously creeps
Climbing the rungs of the skyline
with a cadence
That the wild birds' banter keeps.

I stretch out far and softly groan
Brush the curls out of my purview
Coerce my bones for a finer comb
And rack my mind for abandoned curfews.
The sparrows whisper
sweet jubilance for this morn
Charged with chance and
elbow room—
Adequate for My Ambitions.

The lovers fly assist, aside, asunder
Unshaded, dauntless, and free;

Glide over around and under
(Nay once jilted by humidity).
And the birds' melody fades away
And the wind chimes stir to replace
As tons of ash stroked clouds
lurch to hide the valleys face.
They embezzle the last of the suns gleam
A fixed investment by the dew,
That washes my feet
Where yesterday and tomorrow meet
And makes all familiar things, new.

I admit, I lie, with a sigh,
I do leap!
and in lieu of looking before,
Now and again
I look back.

In the nooks and in the crannies
of my cavernous backup mind,
There are children pulling levers
Who measure the gravity of time.
Mother, Heal me:
In a foot race with discord.
Salt in the air, salt in the water,
Salt of the earth, and salt in the fire,
Thrown out to shore
And taken to the pier, and lacking a lure,
Reading 'Rolling Thunder, Hear me —' Sigh.

I paint these moments as vividly as I can,
A lot of the day I live life, I love life.
I try not to ricochet.

Steeped heavily in the fact that we sought

Milk and honey and found a land of thoughts and
prayers. Thanks Chris.
Gagged by just wanting to be on your
own again.
It's hard to make par and be satisfied.
I'm not even much of a status guy.
Much to my detractor's chagrin.

As the waves break and
Again begin to crest
The sands that slip through my hands
Like the rest
Of the waking hours of my daylight;
I'll do my best.

Staring longingly forward towards
the green light just to press go.
You either have pride or you have nothing:
What's stopping me from going?
I've got a debt to trouble and it
Certainly doesn't share your fortitude.
There aren't ever movies
playing through my head,
and I want to see myself in those lights.
See, the thing about life is
...
You won't be able to live with yourself
for missing out.

There's this dream I keep having, with echoes of you.
Smells warm like honey, where everything is so simple
like glimpses of dimples. And you talk me off the ledge
When I'm being reasonably unreasonable.

A vision worthy of color,
And a visage worthy of wars.
You said satisfied girls don't
Keep with sad boys
So, I conjured joy.

You keep your philosophies on Instagram
And his hopes in her head
'Cuz who knows—
I keep nothing but dust on my shelves
And the animals well-fed.
You're quick to remind me
of the fools in the castle;

I laconically remind you of those without.

You put your memories in a vase
And you water them so they'll bloom
You wear your caprice upon your face.
And never portend or assume.
You flush disappointment down the drain
Pleased with the vista,
and from where you came.
You settle your roots into new soils,
And try on a different name.

In a world where nothing could be
Frayed, broken, or shattered
I had the palatial chance of
Actually sitting beside her.
If you could figure out my feelings
And I could make sense of your time,
Then I could fathom your crucible
And you could accept my crime.
I don't need an understanding
in order to over fall
I think I'm just curious by nature, is all.

Should you measure this life
by glass-half-full moons
And not in the afterglow
Hungover with coffee spoons.
Don't chase the clouds
for they're going a new direction

A thing of doubt, coupled with persuasion;
A vision beyond my wildest creation
Crushes my wiles, leaving me bare and brazen,
And a pitiful modicum closer to you.

The truth that isn't kindness
Is just the skin taut upon the bone.
Moss-covered, weathered stone
A pitiful modicum lighter than you.

Eyelashes like fast passages

in canyons lit by candlelight;
Reticent and grounded
Before I take flight
A pitiful modicum higher than you.

Your irises unshielded
Could level mountains or bore straight through
Uncommonly gilded—
A gaze each day
that seems brand new.

In truth ever present
Halfway between the hallways, & the never,
I listen, exhausted, still thinking I'm clever —
But we're not fooling anyone.

And I hate to be so serious
I don't want this to end, no less soon.
Knowing me, I'm a bit too chivalrous,
To lay prey under paper moons.

I've given my fealty to
The damsel of the blades of grass.
I've gifted her one-of-a-
kind butterfly masks,
And very fine flowers,
And jars full of feathers,
And jams made with stars.
Not to mention the
Numerous pages of
Whimsical balderdash.

She holds court in the ripples of oak roots.
Let these twigs be your scepter
And these sprigs your broach.
I press her nose and she giggles.
And in times of disappointment
Let her look down with a gentle reproach.

And though we are done playing
and Mom wants us home for dinner,
I am a subject first and
a father of grass after.

4
SHE!

You make puddles for us
to play in.

You make puddles for us to play in.
My curiosity rustles through the foliage.
My restless eyes and your restless legs.
Your face sours to see folly, and mine is marred by not
recognizing ours.
Your face isn't drawn into contours today, just the
lighthearted face of youth in cars.
Our love lives large and looms
Over the frivolity, the fickle and
The capricious. It remains casual.

Let us go, pore over this Oak,
Trace every limb above ground and under.
We recognize this bark and the scars cauterized by
Thunder.

The little ones hide in the lower brushes, trying to
remain undetected.
The painter is in the corner
playing to be respected.
And God and bliss is foisted upon
My reluctant Zen friend, because it's possible to be
both seasoned and content. Not only is it possible— it
may be the only way.

Imbued and resolute, in the shade of the clouds where
God hides, and him in the corner, because even
Nature's first green had blue. And curiously disassem-
bled, and longingly eager.
Keep on telling me about the Eskimos,
Where the days are short
and the dreams have indigo.

Behind your heart,
where you've been hiding,
For two hearts diverge
And moved mountains are colliding
And your mind's made up
That you need help deciding.
Apart from your Art,
in this natural lighting.
Although it's miserable in some respects
The crooked times are gentler than I'd expect.
And there's little time to wait
For the field is overgrown and the wind plies and
undulates.
It sparks the memory of her effortless gait, & there's
little more to await.

I press my lips to your collar bone and plant a kiss.
You're the quality of soul,
That mollifies me and unfolds.
As we discuss
The definitions of felicitous or serendipitous
And which word truly best defines us.
And to dream a little dream of you
Is the only thing I truly want to do.

Her eyes were the sun kissed sea
Laid upon cotton-honed moonlight;
Her hair was like a pixie's,
Cowlicked by naps,
And gracious poise was something
She chased out of cats.
Her smile reminds me of the last mile
Of sunlight on the way home from
Playing
Her skin was soft with a lightly tanned tinge, not
weathered or with a lick of decaying:
When Elly first spoke
I had not the foggiest
What she was saying.

But I have patience.

There is history's finest, and then there is I:
A serf, your highness, a speck in the sky.
Rubbish by contrast, with single use sheen
There's a whole world out there
Waiting to be preened.
I traipse this place with grace and aplomb.
Prancing upon buttons, just like your mom.
You and history's finest, say no more!
I'll show you the ladder 'fore
You show me the door.

She

She has a ring full of keys
To answers and antiquities;
She purchased the end of my sentences.
She has a pawn shop, filled with wares,
Worn with cracked paint.
She has no judges,
Cares little for juries,
Needs little counsel,
And bares no fury.
She has sure eyes, certain glasses,
She ponders which vice takes hold the fastest.
And looks me over once to confirm her guess.

She's racing through the cornfield
She's laboring to breathe
Her mind is racing backwards,
From charmed fragility

She's self-possessed and scarred
Her bones are growing weak
Run as she might, she may never outchase
Natural divinity.

She approached with a frenzied rapt,
She's learned more than the morning gods,
Deftly, daftly; yet apt
She vets the dreams that fall under a blind eye
And prods at the embers of our perseverance.

Time and again, I'll tap you on the shoulder
In my sheepish disguise—
And the dawning that you are a wolf,
billows up wide - behind scrupulous eyes.

The Light That Lines Your Eyes!
and the post school laughter
The branch of better reasons
That broke your fall

The day that never dawned
The good cop, bad actors,
The chance of petty treason
That's yours to recall...

The Sun crests craggy skies
the buds dewed up after
The roots of good intentions
You stumbled upon!

Azaleas smattered by design
Spread in the shaded bluff

I'll pick them all for you
But there will never be enough.

She had the visage of
a weak chinned Juliet.
The assured confidence
of a thin nosed Helen,
All her currency wears counterfeit,
With all of the honesty of deliberate,
The worst pitfall I ever fell in.

She had blue hair like Ramona,
Fading out to her natural
Lips that looked as soft as
pillow talk secrets.
Now the trumpets are calling,
And then the whole band kicks in.
And Zelda taps her cigarette case,
Powders her nose and draws her face.

If you married the autumn and the sea, coupled with
the departure of Persephone,
Her hot air balloon eclipses my identity.

And as delighted as Delilah,
And with the consternation of Eve
She needed to be released.

Not from her family and not from a castle,
Not the subject of ridicule or of a vassal—
Not from the war and not from the solace;
A fatally flawed,
Fully contempt
Demi-goddess.
With eyes alike pools of opalescent honey
Let me laze and draw your cunning.

With defiant majesty you, Hester Prynne,
Like Mary Jo, and alike you will sink,
A truculent steward of faith just like Joan
Makes me seem a mannequin, methinks.

Let us meet tonight in the forest
Let's see the other side of
where shadows fall.
— We are not subjects to the leaves,
We are but tourists —
Let us learn this new language
We can shed the old names.
Bury the hatchet by the handle
Tread the old paths and amble
Squeezing topsoil
Between our toes, and
Making the new traditions work for us
Like the old ones never did;
Their growth slowed
And ours blossomed suddenly.
Let us listen to the hum of the katydid chorus
Because tonight will never bore us,
And the past has always been right.

Let us return tonight to the woods,
And sew these shuttered secrets
Amidst the roots,
Riddled with Delight,
And a penchant for the obtuse.

She sought the tree
That bore the fruit
Which time could not decay.
She held court with the Demi-gods,
And in gardens with lesser fae.
She caught the last
Dogwood petal
Dogwood petal
Before it reached the swelter
Once the storm had passed with scorn
And misery no longer compelled her.
She'd been reborn and looking up,
When every utterance said her down.
But once poisoned voices finally shut up,
She took it penny for pound.

Son of an orphan
Drifting
Knowing that all concrete cracks
Eventually
Nobody out there is as alone
And yet incurably,
Nude.
That could be what's happening here, but you'll learn better.
To obviate the debtor,
And purvey the purse.

We'll count the crows until
We grow tired.
Laugh like there's no tomorrow,
And cure yesterday's broken curse.

-

Let me learn it from you —
Mimic your magic.
Be it by the carrot or the stick
I'll learn the dance.

-

You're a boon amongst betters
A bounty for the debtors
With an attitude, both Machiavellian
And millennial,
Vacillating between disappointment
And just a general ennui.
The Goddess of "making it up"
Watching the morning shed away the shadows
She wants my soul,
But she'll settle with my time.
No wiser to her tells
And no worse for wonder.

Alas poor muse,
Tell me what now vexes you?
Deliver me from the shade
of your angelic wing.
No lest as my head lies
restfully upon thine chest
Craft me from
your disappointment
As to shift the mirror-
from blame, I shall winnow thee
from the fear.
Shut the window,
And find a way
to turn me away at the gates,
Like all those other pages
you had dog eared.
And peal my ear —

Prey, that this fleeting despair
is but your eyes flitting towards
An empire that evening has turned back to air
and that the morning mistook
Purpose, for permission.

5
BIG BLUE

Lazarus

I still have yet to see your signal
I'll speak to you now in this moment,
As much visceral.
There will be a time for you
To lean into the breeze,
One to ask the groundskeeper
To leave you the keys.
Sold the farm for a mortgage
And a five-year lease.
Not a single soul, *Est mise en place.*
See the girl with the purple hair?
See how she regrets everywhere?
Me and the kind that care about money
Are completely disparate.
You're dying, remember?
Or am I the one who
Needs to learn the lesson?
No thank you, I've had enough medicine.

And after many committed
Nights of servicing this lighthouse
I still wait for your beacon.
We're toeing our needs to
Spell out our wants,
Est mise en avant.
Don't get lost in the highlight reel.
Maintaining a Porous courage,
Yet the hubris is
Too singed to deal.

Mise en Place

Everyone's got a purpose
I just haven't figured mine out yet.
'Til then, I'll ring lead the circus
And pay off the interest on props debts.
And believe me, I want change—
Tired of seeing a boulevard of broken fangs.
We've run far short of where we should stay
Your senses have been dulled by
too many Mundane Mondays.
We should not lean into the uncertainty
With callous enmity
For in our destiny
It was meant to be.
I'm a peace hound, all too aware
Of the world's pain.
I am raising Cain,
But I am believing Abel.
I mainstream the papistry dream,

And my crusade equipped with a bread knife.
I try to walk through night, if only
To spare what I've suffered through the day
& I don't give a damn what the world may say
Everything is,
Mise en place.

Great Big Blue

A little lazy day would
do us all a great service.
The riddle, told by the
toads and grasshoppers, is
of a speech older than faith.
Something is waiting
just under the surface,
to lift away the weight.

Over yonder beyond Rhythm's bluff,
behind a thinner veil than we're used to;
Feeling hollow and speaking off the cuff,
with withered leaves & half sculpted schemes
Is a lady who makes sprigs bloom, & who Sits the fence betwixt
cadence and creation, murmuring to me,
To never let the hero inside,
become withdrawn, browbeaten to defeat.

Settler, peddler, with a line to cast,
Draw in something pretty from my past.

Somewhere off in to the
great blue distance.
I see the possibilities
I know I'm against.
And that's ok.
When you soak up the water,
You let it all go.
(Drummed up
insight-riddled squatter.
Better than a fiddle player
Stricken in a mental ghetto)

She soaked up the sound,
And I was focused
on where her eyes fell,
And how I can shimmer
And for what it counts
I just want to tell you sometimes.
Somewhere off in the Blue,
Where most of the
weight tries to hide.
I can't litigate your issues,
I can just peer over your fence.
Thrown. Wrench.
Broken. Down. Wall.
When you soak up the water,
You let it all go.
I just want to tell you sometimes.

Somewhere off in to the

great blue distance.
Where time, once, had started.
I saw the end of the circle;
The evidence discarded
And the facts were hurtful.

Somewhere off
in to
the great
blue
distance.
And what goes up
must come down.
We will wash up
beautifully and grounded.

If the first ship sinks, blame the captain;
When the second ship is sunk, blame the crew.

It's laughable, It's laudable
It was not even audible.
Indeterminably casual.
And the movement was lateral.
Initiative is actually
A motive to some;
And when the glass has shattered
And left ripples by design,
And jaggedly numb.

Contrast this
To the pale, grief-stricken nights
Of yonder season
And everything is getting brighter
And light
On its own.
Conjure me, like another one of the ghosts
Remind me again of your splendor
And cough up the wrong Tree
Mingling sweet with the echoes of eternity
Choking filler words, for here,
Modernity
Is uncertainty.

I will ride the darkest horse
I will sheer the blackest sheep
I always dreamt of the blackest dog
Back when I could sleep.
I walk in-between the droplets of the fog
Refuse to get caught, recused, and doused.
I can be your white knight
I can carve out the course
But ne'er shall I ever behold
A pale horse
And all that comes with it.

Incredibly lucky, in the modern sense —
a painter, a monk, a vagabond, & a prince
All attended court to change some minds
Since they've come to
They can't turn back time.

In this schism of opulence
They point fingers, ruminate obscenities
Motives left unquestioned.
Diplomatic indifference
They'll say they struck gold, spark divinity,
The lessons come when beckoned.
'Cuz all they really wanna know
Is what really makes you happy?

Take my hand
Just because — we're here.
Entangled in my fingers
We'll shake this illusion — when it's near.
Between a subject and a predicate
And a jeweled prince of fear.
Take my hand
I'm only satisfied when you are here.
This hour they bud
And tomorrow they blossom
We have our eyes set
Steady, thirsty, and awesome.
You shared your soul with me this night
And you can forever peek into my future.

There's the distance, quite evident,
Between me and you.
We'll bridge it, we can gap it,
Point to where we can overlap it.
There's no facsimile of perfection
There's only what you do.
Have you heard? The poet buds from the roses
Just stop and spell the proses.
And tell 'em all about me
Got nothin' but time.

We are halves of the whole, we will never be asunder, plucked by lightning,
Played by one of those classic plunders.
Nautically feeling evacuated, and before we jump ship,
We kiss like it will be our last
And the way the sunlight
Sprays the water white
Reminds me that we need a dip.

My heart beats in time with this city,
These streets are in my veins,
These capillaries, my vagrant alleys —
These sidewalks will still lead me home.
Crosswalks like shortcuts
And the streetlights flicker
Whenever I shiver.
Your headlights blind me
And peer through this façade.
And my heart seizes
Every time
Another person
Is shot.

6
VICI

God gift me patience,
All the spoils of battle
Will be spoiled by the saddle.
Wooden studs are just the
Bones of a home,
Alas, we're alone
With the froth of the stars and a rattle.

Every town is the same size
Every round is the same price
You either go around quoting scripture
Or you go around carrying the cross.

Tell me your thoughts of the east side.

When the dust has settled
And the breeze right behind it
When your walls have been ravaged
But you're asked to undermine it.
When the lone ship comes in
But the fleet itself is finished.
When your heart's all mucked up,
But you did not truly mind it.
When the mindless minutiae
Leaves the little troubles so unexpected
When you feel so low, so disjointed
A tidbit neglected.
When the day dusks
And you can't tell
What's been measured

Then tell me your thoughts on the east side —
Mercurial and unfettered.

One day you just arrived
Floating adrift on dandelion seeds
The size of hot air balloons.
Eager, clutching the stem
Like it's a streetlight.
Meager! Best yearning;
To be the latter, to meet
The other side of midnight.
And one day you mayhap leave,
And tear drawn eyes mean
Too soon. You'll ferry away
On mammoth-sized daisy petals,
In the form of a pontoon.
Sprinkle sleep
Into the crevices of our eyes —
And beam back at the moon!
One day, when I finally arrived,
Praying on an elephantine Mantis,

Trafficking maps to Atlantis
And wishing
I could always be that Moon.
I know I change just like the tide,
But can I always be that Moon?

The sun steals a peek and it'll lessen
Through the leaves,
And I've dwelled too long in the well;
As the incandescence of the flurries
That dressed the trees,
And it starts to melt;
Today, will be a Beautiful day.

Purpose driven party lines
Credit cards are declined
The tides they are a-changing
And battles outside a-waving
The first one now will later be cast
Back to sea and
Off the shore's shelf.

When all else fails,
Just inhale,
I know I'm alright.
You are peerless,
But it doesn't last forever.
I dreamt I saw, I dreamt that I did,
I dreamt that I was a little kid.

Let's run away now,
just me and you.
We'll build a courtroom
in a patch of bamboo.
Wishes and trysts and butterfly kisses, felicitously
stumble into one another's niches.
I will outline all of your digits,
And then forever will resume.

Secret garden hymns

That we only hear because
We are not like them.
Mountains scream and oceans whisper
The sun beams say I should kiss her.
We dressed up, played catch-up, to one of your treasures
& Worked just long enough for a lifetime of leisure.

We try to hold on to these moments.
Whatever will be, will be.
We dive into these omens
With mud and mortar —
We'll build this up right here,
Serendipitously,
It's meant to be.
And though I will
Yield myself to romance,
I will forever linger in the Circumstance.
Pad lightly along the lily pads,
Cause little to no unrest.

Diogenes and the Case against Nihilism

Prescient lessons, and precious first impressions
Lowers and lessens the fall from grace.
I double checked my work and made some corrections,
remedied all of my mistakes.
I wiped the dust off of the case
And took stock off all of my reflections.
There's nothing worth safekeeping
Quite like your own head above water.

Driven by contrition
And the worst that you take pride in:
Is the hope that you and yours
Are where no one goes, no one could listen.

Covington

The moon shone so bright,
This twilight outside my window,
It turned out to be a streetlight,
Permitting the moon its furlough.
I flipped the shudders
And steered my mind's rudder,
and bore in mind this thought:

Surprise jests and jumps
From thine eyes to mine
Lest yesterday is certain,
Tomorrow is not.

So, I shift back to slumber,
And became unencumbered,
'Til sunlight poured over my window.
With the morning, and my heart awoken,

Life is a circle I prefer to remain unbroken:
And I pour myself into each echo.

Mad with delirium, we wailed into the valley, patiently awaiting its reply.

Oh, sweet nothings!
Come read to me!
Show me around your personal library.
Skip over the volumes bound in misery
Smack off the dust and
Zealously recite the writings
That spell and swell your battered heart!
Breathe sweet, the stories, like Saccharine
To the top of my young lungs again.
The ink doesn't dry once roused,
Titled in golden leaf
Doused in unyielding belief
For a once worn story
Never shrinks with retelling.

I've read the book
About Great Expectations,
Get rich quick
And then go on vacation.
I've read this book
Called *Paradise Lost*
I've been thru hell
And I just hit pause —
No, I just can't take, the heartbreak.

The serpent and the crucible,
(Truculent as ever)
Circle and circumvent
And never waver to sever
From their commitments.
Ouroboros,
Come and consume the end.

They were born this way, worry stroked their mother,
and she quieted her progeny with a prophecy:
There are at least four blind men
who will stand for you —
Two dumb monks who will kneel,
And about three defeated women,
Who will blush —
And always one left to
Read you like a map
Red as the herring

Before it cranes its beak to eat,
Black as the sheep
That you've never cared to hear bleat,
Golden as the child
Like the color hasn't washed out.
Stroke us objects
Abject subjects
Full of purpose
Lest of nothing.
To set my gaze upon your visage
Is my privilege
Soaking up your image
Like the serpent, to the end.

Thirty Diary

I feel the clouds beneath my feet.
I feel like a good dog in heat.
I feel I can't miss another beat —
I feel I'm finally in rhythm.
I feel like a field filled with flowers,
I feel like the eleventh hour.
I feel like all things must pass.
I feel my eyes purvey me
Through the looking glass.

I feel like the jagged edge
Of a broken heart
I feel like a priceless piece of art
I feel like a shell in *Mario Kart*
Just waiting to blow your shit up.
I feel like fighting fire with fire
Opulent and with treadless tires
I feel like a gentleman of desire.

I feel like we'll take it down to the wire
And walk it like a tight rope.
I feel like a paradigm of hope
I feel like political propaganda
Or the unforgiving traffic in downtown Atlanta.
I feel like I'm wasting time...

I feel like a half-used battery
I feel like first impression flattery
Sometimes I feel like an empty lighter,
Full of fuel with a faulty igniter.
I feel like a draft dodger
I feel like the prophet's god father
An infected COVID skeptic
An entire culture
Embedded under water.
I feel like the King James Version,
Half as divine but just as well-spoken.

I feel like snowing at the beach
I feel like I'm just a hair out of reach
I feel like getting lost on purpose
I feel like the ringleader of the circus
I feel just like a belly laugh
I feel like a tepid half full carafe
I feel like a snake,
And then I feel like a dove,
I feel like the definition of Requited Love.
I feel like a lilac in bloom
In the cracks of the pavement.
I feel like a myopic mission statement.
I feel like the Renaissance after the plague,
I feel like the firing line at The Hague.

I feel like Paris at the turn of the century,
I feel like a daily double in Jeopardy.
I feel like I'm where the rubber hits the road,
I feel like the sweat on the brow of Tom Joad.

I feel like the fruit of my labor
I feel like the fruit of my loins
I feel like the right side of the coin.
I feel like the ghost of coal gas,
Gesticulating now, but it's fading fast.
I feel like I'm the last defense
The embodiment of confidence.
I feel myself falling into place perfectly —
And falling right out just as easily.
I feel the world beneath me has begun to shift,
I have stripped the 'why nots' from the 'ifs'.
I feel like the Jack of Hearts,
Held in place by 51 other cards.

I feel like Judy Garland
I feel like Robert Ford
I feel like I'm in a place
Where I cannot be ignored.
I feel like Paul Newman
I feel like Dylan Thomas
I feel like I haven't grown tired
Of trying to be Honest.

I feel like shutters against the storm
The first restless night in my freshman dorm
I feel like the palette of a sunset
I feel like going tête-à-tête.
I feel like a spent gas station

I feel like a respite from a vacation
I feel like a charlatan, I feel like a libertine
I feel like a gardener in the Byzantine.
I feel deliberate and I feel dumb
I've felt everything and now I feel numb.

We're sprawled out under
a bright yellow awning —
You're smiling, I'm laughing
You're stretching, I'm yawning —
And it dawned on me
That this is the last day that I'm thirty.

The facile vassal
And the misanthropic eternity
Man will either get better
Or be off to the infirmary.
& One can't defect,
You must vindicate your part,
Maintain the moral of the story
You — the beating art.
We tip our hats and cheer
& Give it up again
To the new beginning!
Apparently, inherently,
We, the great miracle,
Never over trying
To better our soil,
For in the garden we toil,
In the garden we toil.

ABOUT THE AUTHOR

Elric Wentz is a lover of creating in various mediums — a modern-day Renaissance man. A North Carolina native, Elric can often be found having drinks with friends, playing music, gallivanting outside with his two kids and Huskies, or otherwise keeping his hands and mind busy. Poetry to Elric is a distillation of the beauty in the world into print.

	cuando mi intención supiera.
	Vete con Dios.
Faustino	Plega a Dios
	que no resulte en tu daño.
Leonarda	Vos veréis que no os engaño.
Faustino	Adiós.
Leonarda	Él vaya con vos.
(Vase Faustino.)	He visto a Galindo allí,
	y estábame deshaciendo.
	Darle la caja pretendo
	con el papel que escribí.
	Quiero taparme.
(Tápese con el manto.)	¡Ah, galán!
Galindo	¿Llamáisme?
Leonarda	Sí.
Galindo	¿Qué queréis?
Leonarda	Que a Feliciano le deis
	ciertas cosas que aquí van.
	¿No sois su criado vos?
Galindo	El mismo.
Leonarda	Dadle esa caja.
Galindo	Mucho pesa.

Leonarda	No es de paja. Galindo, adiós.

(Vase Leonarda.)

Galindo	Dama, adiós. ¿Es aquesto encantamento? Mucho el rostro me escondió. ¿Si veré lo que me dio? Pero será atrevimiento. Y viene la caja atada; mejor es llevarla presto. ¡Divinos cielos! ¿Qué es esto? Mas era mujer, no es nada.

(Salen Feliciano, preso y Liseno, caballero.)

Feliciano	Híceos llamar con este pensamiento, y que sobre ese juro me prestásedes los quinientos ducados que suplico; que si de la prisión por vos salieses, no lo dudéis de que en mayor os quedo.
Liseno	Feliciano, si fuera en Madrid nuevo lo que yo suelo hacer por mis amigos, yo os diera aquí satisfacciones largas; pero, como es notorio, las excuso. A Tancredo sacastes de la cárcel, a Rodolfo y Albano; ¿cómo os niegan lo que es tan justo al beneficio mismo?
Feliciano	Por la misma razón pensé obligaros; que, si no de la cárcel, de otras cosas, si la necesidad es harta cárcel,

	os he sacado yo cuando lo tuve.
Liseno	Y yo, si lo tuviera, os acudiera.
Feliciano	Dadme doscientos reales solamente para el procurador que anda en mis pleitos, que he pagado estos días tres fianzas.
Liseno	No los tengo, por Dios, que estoy tan pobre que me presta un amigo, y aun pariente, para lo que es el gasto de mi casa.
Feliciano	Dadme un doblón siquiera, que yo os juro que desde ayer no ha entrado ni un bocado de pan en esta boca que en su vida negó cosa que nadie le pidiese.
Liseno	Aquí traía cosa de ocho reales; éstos tomad, y el cielo, hermano, os libre, que sabe Dios lo que me pesa.
(Vase Liseno.)	
Feliciano	¡Ah, cielos! ¡A un hombre como yo dan ocho reales! ¡Ocho reales le faltan a quien tuvo no ha siete meses treinta mil ducados! Ved qué se cuenta más del mismo pródigo, de Cómodo, Nerón y de Heliogábalo. ¡Ay, si sirviese mi lloroso ejemplo de espejo a los mancebos que me miran, y se guardasen de mujeres tales y de tales amigos!

(Sale Galindo.)

Galindo   No lo digas
                 de burlas.

Feliciano   ¡Oh, Galindo! ¿Aquí escuchabas?

Galindo   Oyendo estaba tus lamentaciones,
                 de que colijo que ninguna cosa
                 hizo por ti Liseno.

Feliciano   Sobre el juro
                 le pedí los quinientos; pero mira
                 en qué se resolvió.

(Enseñándole los ocho reales.)

Galindo   ¡Qué! ¿Esto te ha dado?
                 Guárdale, y clavarémosle a la puerta
                 con una letra alrededor que diga:
                 «Barato que me ha dado la Fortuna
                 de treinta mil ducados que he jugado
                 con los amigos falsos que se usan.»

Feliciano   Bien dices; pero dime, ¿qué responden
                 Fabricio y Dorotea?

Galindo   Entrambos dicen
                 casi una cosa misma.

Feliciano   ¿Estaban juntos?

Galindo   Sí; que, para pagarte el beneficio
                 de librar a su padre de la cárcel,

sirve ya de llevar a Dorotea
galanes que la sirvan y han comido
todos, que, según supe, era un indiano;
Fabricio dice que le diste dados
los dos mil reales, y que agora pides
lo que le distes entonces por fanfarria.
Dorotea responde que los hombres
quieren cobrar de las mujeres luego
aquello con que compran sus placeres.
Que no da nada, y que me guarde.

Feliciano   Dice
muy bien, guárdate de ella. ¡A Dios pluguiera
que me guardara yo!

Galindo   Luego, tras esto,
me dio cierta mujer aquesta caja,
que pesa como plomo aunque es pequeña;
quísela abrir y, por llegar más presto,
ni sé lo que él envía ni yo traigo.

Feliciano   ¡Caja! ¿Qué dices?

Galindo   Ábrela y veráslo.

Feliciano   Corto el cordel que la cubierta enlaza.
¡Quedo, por Dios, que todos son escudos!

Galindo   ¡Salto, bailo! ¡Jesús!

Feliciano   ¡Suceso extraño!

Galindo   Déjamelos besar.

Feliciano	¡Quedo, Galindo! No se te quede alguno entre los labios, porque son pegajosos como obleas.
Galindo	Éstos sí que podrán llamarse amigos.
Feliciano	Aquestos son amigos verdaderos. ¿Quién será esta mujer?
Galindo	Yo sospechara que era Leonarda, a estar mejor contigo; mas dicen que trataba de matarte.
Feliciano	¿Leonarda? ¡Necio! ¿En eso piensa agora, que está amolando espadas, previniendo escopetas con pólvora secreta, confeccionando hechizos y venenos para darme la muerte? Ven, contemos, donde nadie nos vea, estos escudos.
Galindo	¡Oh, amigos verdaderos, aunque mudos!

(Vanse y salen Julio y tres ladrones: Friso, Cornelio, y Friso.)

Julio	Las armas prevenid todos. Pues ya la noche se cierra.
Friso	Yo no sé bien de esta tierra, Julio, las trazas y modos. ¿Hay ronda?
Julio	Agora es temprano.
Lerino	¿Y es ésta la casa?

Julio	Sí.
Lerino	¿Está el capitán aquí?

Julio	Fingióse Marbuto indiano
	   desde Sevilla a Madrid,
	e hizo amistad con un hombre
	que apenas le acierte el nombre,
	y pasa a Valladolid.
	   Llevóle en cas de esta dama,
	que tiene seis mil en oro;
	ha echado el ojo de tesoro,
	que está a los pies de la cama,
	   y quiérele dar gatazo
	mientras la cena apercibe.

Cornelio	Si ése lanza de él se escribe, quedarále dulce el abrazo. ¿Cómo se ha llamado aquí?
Julio	Don Tello.
Lerino	Gracioso nombre.
Cornelio	¿Y está acá también el hombre que ha venido con él?
Julio	Sí.
Cornelio	Eso es peligroso.
Julio	No es, que piensa que es caballero

y hoy gasta lindo dinero.

(Don Tello sale quedo.)

Tello   Julio.

Julio   ¿Qué hay?

Tello   ¿Quién son?

Julio   Los tres.

Tello   ¿Cornelio, Friso y Lerino?

Julio   Los mismos.

Tello   Entro a sacar
el escritorio. Aguardar
podéis.

Julio   ¿Dónde?

Tello   En el camino.

(Vase don Tello.)

Julio   Él ha entrado. Ya es muy tarde;
todo hombre advierta a la cura.

(Salen Feliciano, libre, y Galindo.)

Feliciano   Como hace la noche oscura,
voy, Galindo, algo cobarde,
que ha días que no he pisado

	las calles.
Galindo	Gracias a Dios / que ya nos vemos los dos / en esta esquina del Prado. / Presto trujo el mandamiento / Alberto.
Feliciano	No hay tales pies / como el dinero; al fin, es / el primero movimiento.
Galindo	¿Cuánto la caja traía?
Feliciano	Seiscientos escudos justos.
Cornelio	Estos me han dado mil sustos.
Julio	Este hombre parece espía.
Cornelio	¡Vive Dios, que son criados / de la justicia!
Julio	Yo vuelo.
Friso	Yo, con el mismo recelo.

(Vanse huyendo los tres.)

Galindo	Ciertos hombres embozados / al umbral de Dorotea / van huyendo de los dos.
Feliciano	¿Ya espantamos? ¡Bien, por Dios!

| | ¡Qué habrá que un pobre no sea!
¿Parezco fantasma yo? |
|---|---|

(Sale don Tello.)

Tello	Ce, que digo...
Galindo	Allí nos llama
un hombre, en cas de tu dama.
Feliciano	Lleguemos, si nos llamó.
Tello	Tomad este escritorillo
mientras por el otro voy.
Feliciano (Aparte.)	(¡Bien, por vida de quien soy!)
Tello	Y nadie se atreva a abrillo.
Feliciano (Aparte.)	(¿Conócenos el ladrón?)
Tello	¡Por otros os he tenido!
Que me dejéis ir os pido.

(Húyase don Tello.)

| Galindo | Vaya con la maldición.
Señor, éste es el indiano
que Fabricio trujo acá. |
|---|---|
| Feliciano | Creo que el cielo me da
este castigo en la mano;
bien conozco el escritorio.
Más tiene de siete mil. |

Galindo	¡Qué gentil ladrón!
Feliciano	Sutil. Mi bien es claro y notorio. Éste es todo mi dinero, cuanto a Dorotea he dado. Ved por dónde lo he cobrado.
Galindo	¿Qué has de hacer?
Feliciano	Guardarlo quiero.
Galindo	¿Y si nos encuentra alguno?
Feliciano	¿Allí no vive Leonarda?
Galindo	Sí, señor.
Feliciano	Pues llama.
Galindo	Aguarda.
Feliciano	Mira no te oiga ninguno.
Galindo	¿Si querrá abrir?
Feliciano	¡Plega a Dios!
Galindo	¿Quién está acá?

(Leonarda, dentro.)

Leonarda	¿Quién es?

Feliciano (Aparte.)   (Creo
  que oye el cielo mi deseo.)
  Un preso y dos hombres.

Leonarda   ¿Dos?
  A los dos no puedo abrir;
  al preso, sí. ¡Gloria mía!

(Sale Leonarda.)

Feliciano   Abrevía del alegría,
  que tengo que te decir.

Leonarda   Pues que tú vienes acá,
  alguien te habrá referido
  que mis joyas he vendido,
  o lo adivinaste allá.
    Perdona que yo quisiera,
  como seiscientos le di
  a Galindo...

Feliciano   ¿Tú?

Leonarda   Yo fui.

Feliciano   ¡Pero quién sino tú fuera!
    Débote mi libertad,
  el alma misma te debo.
  Hoy me obligaste de nuevo;
  mas oye una novedad.

(Ruido dentro.)

Galindo	Gritos dan, éntrate dentro.

(Dorotea, dentro.)

Dorotea	¡Traidor Fabricio, tú fuiste quien a casa le trujiste!
Leonarda	¿Qué es esto?
Feliciano	Un gracioso encuentro. De la puerta de esa dama, que mi hacienda me robó, salió un ladrón que le hurtó el dinero y no la fama. Topó con nosotros dos, por compañeros nos tuvo, y éste nos dio, que no estuvo en un instante, por Dios, de dar con los verdaderos. ¡Mira por dónde he cobrado cuanto con ella he gastado!
Leonarda	Sin duda son tus dineros. Acá viene gran ruido. Allá le voy a esconder.
Galindo	El dinero has de verter en otro, sin ser sentido y échale luego en el pozo.
Leonarda	Voy; aquí a la puerta aguarda.

(Vase Leonarda.)

Feliciano	¡Qué contenta va Leonarda! Yo estoy saltando de gozo.

(Salen un Alguacil, y gente que traiga asido a Fabricio. Salen también Dorotea y Clara.)

Fabricio	¿Pues a mí preso? ¿Por qué?
Alguacil	Porque es muy bastante indicio para prenderos Fabricio.
Fabricio	Vive Dios, que no lo sé.
Dorotea	Trújole él propio a mi casa, y con él se concertó, ¿y no le conoce?
Fabricio	¿Yo?
Galindo	Ved lo que en el mundo pasa.
Clara	Yo juraré que es ladrón, y que a don Tello encubría, que desde el Andalucía trujo para esta ocasión. Él sabía del dinero; él le dijo dónde estaba.
Fabricio	¿Yo le truje?
Clara	Y le abonaba de indiano y de caballero.
Dorotea	Gente hay en aquesta puerta.

	¿Quién va?
Feliciano	Un hombre que ha salido de la cárcel.
Alguacil	¿No habrá sido el ladrón?
Feliciano	Cosa es bien cierta.
Alguacil	¿Es el señor Feliciano?
Feliciano	Yo soy.
Alguacil	Por mil años sea.
Feliciano	¿Qué es esto de Dorotea?
Dorotea	¿Agora estáis cortesano? Vaya a la cárcel Fabricio.
Alguacil	Que Fabricio le ha robado un escritorio, o ha dado de que fue cómplice indicio, porque le trujo un indiano que ha sido el cierto ladrón; siete mil escudos son.
Feliciano	Esos son de Feliciano.
Alguacil	¿Habéis visto estos ladrones?
Feliciano	Solo a Galindo y a mí.

Alguacil	Juradlo aquí.
Feliciano	Juro aquí que he sentido esos doblones, y aun que los he visto puedo jurar.
Dorotea	¡Que éste se ha vengado!
Clara	¡Cuál están amo y criado!
Fabricio	¿Yo soy ladrón?... ¡Bueno quedo! Diga Feliciano aquí si sabe que soy ladrón.

Feliciano	Quien paga amor con traición,
	ladrón es; digo que sí.
	   Quien niega deudas tan claras
	y no paga el beneficio,
	¿de ser ladrón no da indicio?
	Pues, ladrón, ¿en qué reparas?
	   Vete, que lo juro y digo
	que en ésta y toda ocasión
	sustentaré que es ladrón
	quien es traidor al amigo.
	   Y que del dinero hurtado
	a Dorotea, quisiera
	que dos veces tanto fuera,
	por la ingratitud que ha usado;
	   y que a estar en mi poder,
	no me diera más contento,
	y que de mi casamiento
	testigos os quiero hacer.
	   ¡Leonarda!

(Sale Leonarda.)

Leonarda ¿Señor?

Feliciano Yo soy
tu esposo; sea testigo
un ladrón e infame amigo,
a quien este ejemplo doy;
   una dama cortesana
y una criada fingida
que roban toda la vida
con industria loca y vana,
   para que tras años mil
vuelvan las aguas a donde
solían ir, pues ya lo esconde
cierta mano más sutil;
   y un alguacil también sea
testigo de que me caso,
y sepa que no hago caso
del amor de Dorotea
   porque si algún aire infame
me quisiere hacer prender,
sepa que tengo mujer
y que así a Leonarda llame.
   Doyle en dote siete mil
ducados que ha recibido;
testigos, pues que lo han sido
el dueño y el alguacil;
   y a Galindo, por leal,
toda mi hacienda le doy.

Galindo Yo señor tu esclavo soy.

Fabricio	¡Paga de quien anda en mal!
Dorotea	Llévalde a la cárcel luego.
Alguacil	Digo que gocéis mil años, pues ya de tantos engaños venís a tanto sosiego. Tómela de la mano.
Feliciano	¡Adiós, señores testigos! Y aquí Belardo dio fin a una historia, que es, en fin la prueba de los amigos.

Fin de la comedia

Libros a la carta
A la carta es un servicio especializado para
empresas,
librerías,
bibliotecas,
editoriales
y centros de enseñanza;
y permite confeccionar libros que, por su formato y concepción, sirven a los propósitos más específicos de estas instituciones.
Las empresas nos encargan ediciones personalizadas para marketing editorial o para regalos institucionales. Y los interesados solicitan, a título personal, ediciones antiguas, o no disponibles en el mercado; y las acompañan con notas y comentarios críticos.
Las ediciones tienen como apoyo un libro de estilo con todo tipo de referencias sobre los criterios de tratamiento tipográfico aplicados a nuestros libros que puede ser consultado en Linkgua-ediciones.com.
Linkgua edita por encargo diferentes versiones de una misma obra con distintos tratamientos ortotipográficos (actualizaciones de carácter divulgativo de un clásico, o versiones estrictamente fieles a la edición original de referencia).
Este servicio de ediciones a la carta le permitirá, si usted se dedica a la enseñanza, tener una forma de hacer pública su interpretación de un texto y, sobre una versión digitalizada «base», usted podrá introducir interpretaciones del texto fuente. Es un tópico que los profesores denuncien en clase los desmanes de una edición, o vayan comentando errores de interpretación de un texto y esta es una solución útil a esa necesidad del mundo académico.
Asimismo publicamos de manera sistemática, en un mismo catálogo, tesis doctorales y actas de congresos académicos, que son distribuidas a través de nuestra Web.
El servicio de «libros a la carta» funciona de dos formas.
1. Tenemos un fondo de libros digitalizados que usted puede personalizar en tiradas de al menos cinco ejemplares. Estas personalizaciones pueden ser de todo tipo: añadir notas de clase para uso de un grupo de estudiantes,

introducir logos corporativos para uso con fines de marketing empresarial, etc. etc.

2. Buscamos libros descatalogados de otras editoriales y los reeditamos en tiradas cortas a petición de un cliente.

www.ingramcontent.com/pod-product-compliance
Lightning Source LLC
Chambersburg PA
CBHW051343040426
42453CB00007B/392